SEAN JUAN
CANTO 1

JACK HOLLAND

PUBLISHED BY
LAPWING PUBLICATIONS
c/o DENNIS & RENE GREIG
1 BALLYSILLAN DRIVE
BELFAST BT14 8HQ

TYPESET BY
LAPWING GRAFIX
c/o BRIAN CHRISTIE
51 KILCOOLE GDNS
TELE: 712483

ISBN 1 898472 10 6

LAPWING POETRY PAMPHLET
Jack Holland: Sean Juan Canto 1
PUBLISHED 1994
COPYRIGHT REMAINS WITH AUTHOR

Lapwing Publications gratefully acknowledge the financial assistance of the **Arts Council of Northern Ireland** and **The UK Foundation for Sport and the Arts** in the publication of this pamphlet.

AN INTRODUCTION TO SEAN JUAN.

Sean Juan first appeared in extract in the magazines Hibernia and Threshold. That was almost twenty years ago. Now, at last, I have the gratification to see it published in full, in two parts, for the first time.

For me, Sean Juan was many things: an act of homage to Lord Byron; an indulgence in the pleasure of writing a verse form for the sheer enjoyment of that form; and, perhaps most importantly, an act of rebellion against self-righteousness and smugness which have deformed so much of Irish -- and in particular Northern Irish -- life.

Sometimes I look upon Sean Juan as a youthful indiscretion in verse. But twenty years after I began my career as a professional writer it is one that I still recognise as my own.

Rome Italy.   12th July, l994.

For Mary
Sagest of women, and of wives the best.
(The first part's Byron's, but mine's the rest.)

Canto 1

PART 1

I have a hero - problem is, his place of birth.
Of such a place the poet never sings;
Of all the cities on this planet Earth
It seems the timid Muse never <u>that</u> way wings.
Of lyrics, sonnets, odes, there's been a dearth.
Poor bard! Can he be blamed if down he flings
His pen, and instead of edifying verses
On Belfast heaps an anthology of curses?

Yet, I shall refrain from railing at her.
There Sean Juan was born, below the drumlin
Hills of Down, by lovely Lagan's water.
Specifically, the place they put his mum in
Was an ancient hospital - The Mater,
Next door to the jail they call The Crumlin;
And she distinguished them, because the nuns
Who nursed the mothers, didn't carry guns.

There his mother lay for weeks 'til well past
The day that he was due. But warm as toast
Within the womb, happy there he held-fast
'Til Derby Day. As the winner passed the post
Ass-ways first they backed him into Belfast -
That is the part of him his ma remembers most.
This was a sight gave rise to some dismay:
Mother Nature pointed Juan the other way

As if to show her contempt for the place.
And this was how our hero made his start;
We cannot say he put on a brave face -
In fact, his only comment was to fart,
To which the nuns replied with a grimace,
Making their sour faces look more tart.
"Here is," thought they, the Sisters of Mercy,
"A bundle of potential heresy."

So when poor Juan was ready for inspection,
The nuns, who'd gathered round the cot,
Examined every limb, with due reflection,
To see what kind of creature God'd begot,
If it was capable of genuflection,
And holding beads and kneeling down and
    what-not,
All things good Catholics would expect,
But one: something was surprisingly erect!

The nuns stood back and wrung their hands,
    aghast.
That was an organ for which they had no use,
(The sight of one entailed a ten day fast);
They'd heard that it was prone to much abuse,
Especially in a city like Belfast,
And knew it was in conflict with their views,
Bore no resemblance to the Holy Ghost,
The method which the Church admires the most.

Perhaps until that day the nuns had thought
That mother Ireland was entirely free
From snake-like things (that tempt them with a bad
    thought),
Assuming they'd been chased into the sea,
With Reds and reptiles, and all who had sought
To lift our isle out of the Holy See,
Thanks to Ireland's Patron Saint, Saint Patrick,
When he performed his justly famous hat-trick.

The nuns turned to his mother to admonish;
Her marriage really wasn't very sound.
Her husband's ancestors - this will astonish
And all the nuns and doctors did astound -
Were foreigners; in fact, they were all Spanish,
Who in 1584 had run aground
Not far from here. After a famous hassle
One Juan was washed ashore near Ballycastle.

He settled there. Bid addios to courts and balls.
Centuries passed by. The Juans went all
Down to Belfast - foolishly, Sean recalls.
The oldest made a match, experimental:
He married an Italian from the Falls
Who owned a chip-shop called the Continental.
There, to help hold down their beer and whiskies
The Falls Road men get their chips and pisces.

Meanwhile Mrs. Juan slept on, encircled by the
    nuns,
Unconscious of the stir her son had made.
"Your son's behaviour really rather stuns
Us all," they said. "For his morals we're afraid,
Mrs. Juan. You know the risk a woman runs
Married to a foreigner. Has your husband ever
    prayed?"
They knew the French, the Spanish and the
    Flemish
Never climb Croagh Patrick or Mount Slemish.

A brief diversion, for I must explain
That these two hills are where the Irish,
When in need of a little extra pain
To suffer for their sins, like to perish;
But most often they are let off with a sprain.
Every minor bruise they're taught to cherish,
Their spiritual experience for to heighten,
Which can't be done in Bangor or in Brighton.

It was a scene strange in the extreme,
For Mrs. Juan was roused by the alarm
From the middle of her very pleasing dream;
She'd been dreaming of her husband's Latin charm
As he was handing her a large ice-cream
Contained in a cone. "A second one will do no
    harm,"
Thought she when by the sudden noise awoke
And sat up saying "Juan, give us another poke."

She hadn't heard a word of what the nuns had said,
And they stood back, blushing in confusion.
Across their faces there passed a look of dread,
That showed what they'd perceived in her effusion –
The meaning that their subtle minds had read;
Obviously a Freudian allusion.
In such allusions, about which Freud spoke,
A pig is not a pig, nor a poke a poke.

Yet, it's not a subject for a frolic,
Nor something to be talked of in a jest.
Many women dwell on things symbolic;
By day and night it never gives them rest.
All upright things to them are downright phallic.
I feel they're far too easily impressed.
Just think of this - especially if prone - :
Imagination is an erogenous zone.

Yet Mrs. Juan was hardly one of those.
Indeed, she'd never even heard of Freud,
Or spent much time trying to diagnose
Her dreams, or analyse things which she enjoyed -
Like looking at a fireman with a hose.
The minds of Irish girls are otherwise employed,
Except for subtle ladies like the nuns,
Always seeing ambiguities and puns.

Take the famous story which goes thus.
Singing in a choir, little Sister Anne is
Distracted from her hymn, "Panis Angelicus",
By St. George's picture - a saintly man is
Still a man. Before long there's a fuss.
The word that she is singing isn't "panis"!
Indeed, it takes us back where we began,
To a little organ, and a little Juan.

The nuns agreed. With such precocity
The boy should be removed. They push his cot,
Sometimes with frightening velocity,
To somewhere sheltered - a distant spot
Picked out with moral animosity,
As far from baby girls as could be got.
Hence Sean's sense of loneliness, appalling,
Which in this instance he expressed by bawling.

So they prepare the crises of the years to come,
So ruling many lives from pram to hearse.
But now I have to take Sean and his mom
Out of the hospital, so I must be terse.
Her husband came one day and took her home.
(A serviceable line, if not great verse.)
They gladly said goodbye to the Mater,
And went to live with her husband's pater.

End Of Part 1

PART 2.

The slums are always with us, high and low;
The oul Pound Loney or the Divis Towers,
It makes no difference how far up we go
Little we see around us will be ours.
But still, the streets are snugger, this we know.
Above the winds howl round us at all hours!
Great God! I'd rather be a weed among the cobbles
Than a leaf upon a tree that wobbles.

Our hero now was such a little weed
As grows between the back streets of the Falls,
Where he learned the skills he'd later need.
By studying the slogans on the walls
Our Belfast hero even learned to read
Those pithy maxims that he still recalls.
Except for one, with which he'd have no truck.
Who'd want to **** the Queen? (I fear the censor
    struck.)

Such slogans then, our Sean knew all about.
But soon his mind sought greater stimulation,
So something which he could have done without
He got - a Christian Brothers' "education".
(Education here means "manys a clout",
And Christian? - That requires a revelation.)
What was their founder called? I think he had
A name like De la Salle. Or De la Sade?

As when first a prisoner sees his guard,
So Juan looked up in horror at St. Gall's;
Its windows were all stained, and dark, and barred,
Its gates were like a prison's, and its walls;
The playground too was like a prison yard
Around which the hopeless chaingang daily crawls.
So Sean's heart sank, as did his mother's,
When he was marched off by the Christian
    Brothers.

Sean was to their tender care entrusted
Just before he reached the age of seven.
His teacher's name was Brother Maladjusted,
Who'd chose the long and bumpy road to heaven,
Paved with all the little heads he'd busted.
And every day, until he was eleven,
Sean counted every bruise he gave, and crack,
Enough to take his teacher there and back.

Now Maladjusted sought to emulate
The Head - Big Brother as they called him, Flayum,
Whose rulings on how best to educate
The young were all applied, and with aplomb,
By Brothers on their bottom, hands and pate.
Apart (of course) from Brother Ticklebum,
The staff were all exceedingly expert
In everything and anything that hurt.

In order to deter the would-be sinner
Flayum sought and found a modern saviour,
Unearthed the doctrines of Professor Skinner -
"Scientific Theories of Behaviour" -
Who discovered rats work harder for their dinner.
The Head required a modern flavour for
His work. More effective are whacks, you see,
Applied with scientific accuracy.

The Brothers, they were moving with the times.
No longer would they ever have recourse
To terms like "right", "wrong", "punishment", or
    "crimes",
Now instead they took a vow to <u>reinforce</u>
Boys with Operant Conditioning Paradigms,
With lots and lots of stimulus, of course.
They applied it with as much precision
As Behaviourists of old, the Inquisition.

Their method was quite simple and discerning.
"Give me a cane," said Flayum, "and a fact.
That's the combination known as learning.
Show me a skull that can't be cracked,
Into which a little Truth concerning
Faith, Morals, Obedience, can't be packed.
I don't believe that such a thing exists!"
He'd shout, while shaking both his fists.

But Ticklebum, he was the real trend-setter
Of the school, asserting he was there to "please"
The little boys, and that they'd learn much better
If only he could stroke their little knees.
"I am your pupil. I am your indebtor,"
He'd stress, "very like an Irish Socrates."
O what if there had been an Irish Plato?
There's food for thought (like the potato).

Though no Plato, nor an Aristotle,
Was there to listen to this wise man speak,
His class preferred a tickle to a throttle,
And cared not if its origins were Greek,
Leaving him to gaze into his ink-bottle.
And when he sighed - struck by his plight so bleak -
"If only I'd been born Athenian,"
They thought, "He's nuts - of course he's a Fenian."

But for Sean the book of history was shut,
Except between the Famine and the Rising,
As that was Maladjusted's well-greased rut,
Greased with the blood of all his heros, comprising
O'Connell, Patrick Pearse and Mat Talbot.
Though Daniel lost no blood (that's not surprising)
Poor Matthew lost enough for three or four,
Regretting at his death he'd not lost more.

Such agony! Tortures such would flatter
An Irish saint! He chose to suffer for <u>our sins</u>,
(That no one asked him didn't seem to matter).
He wrapped himself in chains from head to shins,
And then collapsed, making quite a clatter,
Like the clanging of a dozen empty bins.
I think the reason that poor Matthew fainted -
He hoped that one day soon he would be sainted.

But saints these days are few and far between,
That is, compared to 1924,
When Mr. Talbot was last on the scene.
Recently we've seen a dozen saints or more
Reduced, each one, to a heavenly has-been.
I'm sure they must be feeling rather sore,
Regretting time spent at their communion,
Instead of building up a good trade union.

Maladjusted held up Mat's example
And hoped his little boys would be inspired,
But Sean believed his sufferings were ample,
Enough to get to heaven, as required.
Of hell he felt he'd already had a sample.
A little paradise was what our Sean desired.
But where was that? Looking from St. Galls,
The nearest heaven seemed outside its walls.

It can't be said Sean flourished as a scholar.
Indeed, it seems the opposite is true.
Some things he did learn well: how to hollar
As he was beaten daily black and blue.
He wished each Brother hung up by his collar,
And day by day this pleasing fancy grew.
Then after seven years he was able
To remember that "an tabla" meant "the table".

So little knowledge our hero had to carry!
But some few facts he knew, and several tricks,
Like "Londonderry" was in fact spelt "Derry",
Ulster was really nine and not just six,
That (and here the arithmetic gets very
Deep) six will soon go into 26,
Then (defying laws of division) you
Will find the final answer: 32!

But others (mainly from the other side)
Have added yet a further complication.
They calculate (but only to divide)
The six must equal one whole nation.
In fact, it only turns the problem inside
Out - now who can solve the explanation?
This little theory has some affinity
To the maths of the Blessed Trinity.

We'll leave all this to Irish calculus,
Which seems especially set-up to defy
All mathematics' laws, confusing us.
Just look at how they easily get by
Without the use of minus or of plus:
It seems the Irish only multiply.
Enough! No more of maths, because Dear Reader,
My Muse must dash, and numbers just impede her.

We've still to get Sean to another school,
And though just up the road a mile or so,
From St. Galls its a long way to have to pull
A verse like this, with eight long lines in tow.
Excuse me then, for I must break a rule
And get us there at once, all in one go.
This phase of Sean's life we will define as
"Steeled in the school of old Aquinas."

Sean's new school was named after Aquinas;
There older boys were sent, too poor to chose.
His education wasn't quite as fine as
Joyce's, with his Jesuitical muse;
Here Sean was to learn the taste cheap wine has,
To pick a lock, break a head, - and self-abuse.
Since one's self was abused by every other
One may as well abuse it as another.

This is quite a common sin, I think you'll find,
In spite of all the nonsense clerics spout,
Who claim too much of it will make you blind,
Your blood curdle and all your hair fall out,
Your toes curl, teeth rot, and derange your mind,
Wreck your nerves and all your seven senses rout.
But still the clergy's gloomy promises
Went unheeded by the boys in St. Thomases.

It was the sort of place that was designed
To prepare the pupils for their future role.
Indeed, a better place it would be hard to find
To prepare you for a life time on the dole,
A life time making do with just the rind
Of life - because the fruit was not your goal.
It's still the same, and still to get the fruits
You have to tear the tree up by its roots.

St. Thomas's was built beside the Blackie,
A little stream that flowed through old Belfast.
Sweet-watered as the sweat off a lackey,
As wholesome as a trench that's just been gassed,
As pleasant as the smell of stale tabaccy,
As healthy as the plague-pits of the past.
The old boys took the new, as was the custom,
And in its gurgling, limpid waters, thrust 'em.

But Sean escaped such fate, and this is why.
He noticed most of those who got the wetting
Were well dressed up in blazer, badge and tie,
Which all the older Thomists found upsetting,
Who saw life, by this time, more cynically.
Our hero then was very fast in getting
Rid of all his more polite apparel,
Which he concealed nearby, inside a barrel.

At first he tried a swagger, looking tough,
Hoping to discourage interference.
Instead of which - poor Sean - they called his bluff,
And made him wish that he could disappear hence;
The older Thomists tended to be rough -
Rough and mean, the foes of mere pretence,
Ulster heros, not inclined much to talk,
Who'd rather slaughter armies, or scoop out a
    lough.

At St. Thomas's our Sean learned other facts,
What might be called a "liberal" education,
Or what Eliot, the poet, called "brass tacks",
Of birth and death, but mainly copulation,
Most conflicting with the Church's view that sex
Was only to increase population.
And soon its threats of hell and mortal sin
(The price of lust) but made him yawn or grin.

"The expense of spirit in a waste of shame
Is lust in action", wrote you know who -
My rhyme cannot accommodate his name -
But in St.; Thomas's this simply wasn't true.
There the lack of action we should blame.
If boys were mad, extreme and savage too,
The reason wasn't lust at all; rather, no man
Is at his best without a girl or woman.

Sean listened as the anxious clergy thundered
About the dangers in "Occasions Of Sin",
And asked himself, as he sat and wondered,
"When are these occasions going to begin?
How long will I have to Wait?" he pondered.
By 15 his hopes were wearing thin.
Dear Reader - do not fret as much as he;
I promise you seduction in Part Three.

End Of Part 2.

PART 3.

In spite of all abuse that's laid upon her
Sweet Belfast has a charm that's all her own.
Of no place could a man be fonder:
The Falls, the Pound, the Markets and the Bone,
Heroic names that make one stop and ponder,
For History's left her mark on every stone;
And every stone its mark on History too -
In fact, they've beaten History black and blue.

I mention this - a pleasant introduction -
Unrelated to what follows; do not vex,
But before the promised stanzas on seduction,
The "joys" of adolescent love and sex,
And the tale of our hero's first induction
Into those arts which prompt a poet to wax
Lyrical, for instance - Shelley, Burns, or Keats,
I'll warn how sex is thought of in those streets.

The entries are too small that could be bigger,
Making love upon a bin rarely succeeds,
With a woman only worth a snigger.
What is she in the Church's feudal creeds
(And after all, the Church is her grave-digger)?
A creature that is beaten, breathes and breeds.
When choice occurs - her breeding or her breath?
The Church has made it. She breeds herself to
    death.

To call their doctrines feudal is unfair.
Their roots in fact go back to the Dark Ages,
When Christians made a doctrine of despair.
To the deserts thronged distracted sages,
Guilt-ridden; some took to caves and grew their
    hair,
Some took to pillar tops, and some to cages,
And some, like Origen, in mad frustration,
Sought to rid themselves of man's sensation.

Let's not forget that ex-rake St. Augustine.
He said that "Women should love chastity,
Then their husbands" - "holy vessels" they've trust
    in.
That sex could be enjoyed, he thought a pity;
After many youthful years of lustin'
Round every whore-house in that Ancient city,
"In Carthage then I came", he might well write,
Who came in Carthage nearly every night.

I fear his ghost still haunts the Catholic bed,
Although he died in A.D. 430.
"Sexual passion is full of shame", he said.
So when the Irish male takes off his shirt he
Makes sure the lights switched off in holy dread -
For what is done, he knows, is very dirty,
In Carthage, Belfast or in Ancient Rome,
Ridden by guilt in brothel or at home.

Attend awhile the Catholic male, half bare:
Leaps into bed - but oops, that is, <u>not quite</u>,
Gets out again - he still must say his prayer,
Then rises, having finished - a thrilling sight,
And with determination climbs in where
His wife lies waiting. Her face glows in the light
That burns above their bed amid a throng
Of Angels - a Sacred Heart made in Hong Kong;

(Its iridescent glow is guaranteed).
On the walls are other Catholic wares
Placed 'round the room to oversee the deed:
The Virgin Mary from a corner stares
To supervise the spending of the seed;
Pope Pius too upon the couple glares
Next to where the Apostles' Creed is pasted,
To make sure not a single drop is wasted.

Not wasted, for as Mother Church's stated,
Intercourse, (which after all, God <u>did</u> invent)
Is merely to ensure we're procreated.
But should a sperm escape with bad intent,
Just as the sacred act is consummated,
As fast as moves good news from Aix to Ghent,
Such proof that sex can really be enjoyed
Would leave their sick restrictions in a void.

Ottava Rima's gone off on its rambles,
And left our hero some ten stanzas back.
The Picaresque prefers the bush and brambles
To the narrative's well-beaten track,
But runs the risk of ending in a shambles,
Unless the poet has a good back-pack
That's full of pithy matter, shall we say,
To keep the reader nourished on the way.

The point was Juan, hero of this poem.
His frustration by now was not surprising.
I gave the reasons - the Irish well know 'em.
By 16 his temperature was rising,
And boys, so Mother Nature likes to grow 'em,
Are at that age much given to despising
Whatever laws are meant to hold them back
From doing that for which they have the knack.

And so Sean Juan became an atheist,
Abandoned Church and Faith, all in one go.
Though he thought that God could not exist
He dodged about, expecting a lightning blow.
Thought or not, superstitions still persist;
Our feelings lag behind the things we know:
The mind runs far ahead in all its knowing,
But the feelings on all fours make slower going.

Avoiding mass, Sean would grace the park where
He'd sit and think of girls beneath the trees.
He'd think of bumping into Rosie Parker,
And bumps with her were really meant to please;
He'd think of sitting next to Fanny Larker,
Whose reputation sailed the seven seas.
On such he mused, beneath the boughs so
   splendid,
Until he judged the noon-day mass had ended.

So many a dreary Sunday passed away,
Through Winter-time beneath the basalt hills,
When Divis Mountain loomed a misty grey,
When rolling clouds the Lagan Valley fills.
Our hero would give in to deep dismay,
Shivering in a shelter from the chills.
I think the poem's gone too melancholic;
It's time to introduce a little frolic.

It happened on a Sabbath late in May.
The daisy clusters all around the green
Were bright as stars upon the Milky Way,
The buttercups shone with the Summer's sheen.
In fact, the Falls was looking rather gay -
As gay, that is, as it had ever been.
Our hero moped alone beneath the trees,
"His hair soft lifted" by the Summer breeze.

He watched old men play bowls upon the green,
Not far from where the Blackie gurgled by.
Suddenly, this quaint and pastoral scene
Was broken by a pained and angry cry -
And one old man lay stretched as if he'd been
Felled by a thunderbolt from out the sky.
Such heavenly events were not to blame -
Rather, another bowler'd missed his aim.

He'd seen a sudden sight that made him flinch,
And entirely put his game out of mind,
A sight all eyes soon followed - inch by inch.
It passed, and then the sight was all behind.
And though "behind" indeed was Glenda Pinch,
A more forward girl it would be hard to find.
These are merely Nature's contradictions,
Allowing us to pun without restrictions.

Glenda came from Glasgow every summer
To celebrate the Battle of the Boyne.
Though to Belfast she was no new-comer
She'd gotten lost whilst on her way to join
Her uncle's band. He was a Lambeg Drummer,
"A Loyal Son and Bold", if I may purloin
A famous phrase of those who sing the wonders
Of King Billy, and scorn King James' blunders.

She'd found herself instead upon the Falls.
Don't ask me now how Glenda went astray,
As far from her beloved Orange Halls
As if along the shores of Galway Bay.
Had she but read the writings on the walls
Without mischance she would have found her way.
Perhaps it was decreed above by fate
That she'd turn left instead of going straight.

Now Glenda up the Falls made quite a splash
(The thought would make an Orange lily wilt),
A shock of colour was her Orange sash,
And as she walked she wagged her tartan kilt,
Which gave the Falls a very orange flash -
A sight for which in Glasgow blood was spilt.
But taig or prod, thought she, "what's in a name?"
For Glenda held all men were much the same.

Now there's a point of view one could defend -
(But when a man held Glenda, could he doubt it?)-
Her facts were those on which you could depend.
Thanks, I say, for female tact, without it
Many's a cocky male would meet his end.
Instead of which he's free to boast about it.
(Some men are even said to keep a score.
For women, counting men would be a bore.)

A woman's "place", of course, will always mould
    her.
For while the hero's face is in the pillow
She looks out on things over his shoulder,
And sees some sights that he will never know.
Unless, that is, the pair are somewhat bolder,
But all the combinations I'll forego.
Had we but world enough and time - how fine
To list them all from one to 69.

A stanza for each one might be enough,
Although to each I could devote a canto,
For making love is hot poetic stuff -
An epic's length attain, if I'd want to.
And should the reader think I merely bluff,
Let him read on. I promise he'll pant who
Reads another verse - or two. No mere pretext
To get us from this stanza to the next.

By such strange ways our heroine had come
To meet Sean Juan - still propped against the bark.
He watched her, listening for the Lambeg drum,
As she marched by him through the quiet park.
And as she went she seemed to wag her bum,
A thing on which I think I should - remark.
Imagine two round hillocks of smooth sand
Swaying to the rhythm of an Orange band.

By now you understand what made men stare.
Such pleasure in poetic pains, I've found,
So imagine something shaped round like a pear -
One that's just ripe for plucking, I'll be bound.
(Taste not the fruit before the branch is bare.)
Glenda's path was circular, one that wound
To where Juan sat, feeling quite forgotten,
That when he got the fruit it might be rotten.

When Glenda saw our hero looking on -
He had a face which any girl could trust -
She stopped, looked up, and pointing, said
"Where's thon?
If a don't get to the Shankill soon, a'll bust."
"That there's the cemetery," replied our Sean,
"A short-cut to the Shankill which is just
A mile or so beyond the other gate.
You'll want to hurry though - it's gettin' late."

But Glenda was, in spite of her aplomb,
Timid in graveyards, surrounded by the dead.
And Juan, who sensed this - he was far from
    dumb -
Thought that - if - perhaps - she might - like to be
    led
And Glenda thought that if the youth could come,
Then all her fears she'd very quickly shed.
So when our hero offered for to guide her
She felt relieved - that is, deep down inside her.

The new found friends had first a wall to climb.
For this our Glenda needed quite a shove,
So Juan got round behind her just in time,
Held her firm below 'til she was above,
And what he felt - I truly doubt mere rhyme
Can forcefully convey the feeling of.
At times like this the plastic art's a must -
Words melt inside the furnaces of lust.

He raised her slowly, only by degrees.
Once up, our hero followed close behind
'Til both stood trembling in the gentle breeze
That lifted Glenda's tartan skirt to find
The only wafting needed was a sneeze.
(For what else now are women's skirts designed?)
Like he who touched the hem of Nature's shift,
Sean Juan felt faint, for that was quite a lift.

Before them stretched the silent cold graveyard,
In gathering gloom, where many souls are laid,
As Sean recalled. His heart was beating hard.
The same dark thought had Glenda quite dismayed.
In he leapt, to show he was no coward.
Glenda hovered on the edge, then displayed
Her finest qualities: she gave a shriek
And fell upon our hero, so to speak.

Sean was, shall we put it, laid - but not to rest,
Merely stunned and stretched out in the grass.
Gasped Glenda, fumbling still upon his chest,
"I felt a boney finger touch my ass."
You might well say our hero was impressed
To see his dreams converted into mass.
No formula devised my Mister Planck
Describes the mass beneath which Sean Juan
    sank.

Of boney fingers now there is some doubt.
Perhaps a twig had caused this happy clinch?
But just in case, our hero felt about
With his warm hands to calm the frightened Pinch,
The kind of warmth one can not do without;
And Glenda, though brought up on "Not an Inch",
At such times ignored that petty measure:
No inch'd ever part her from her pleasure.

So there was Sean Juan and Glenda lay entwined.
Some readers now may shun this with abhorrence,
Who think the poet should draw down the blind.
To them, of course, it's such a rare occurrence,
And then occurs more often in their mind -
The "mental sex" condemned by D. H. Lawrence.
I'm saddened that some readers are outraged
By honest poems on lovers so engaged.

Poor Juan, poor Juan - he'd had so long to wait.
His state may be described as kind of "virgin",
Not self-imposed, but rather due to fate,
From which the lad was eagerly emergin' -
By this stage in our tale at such a rate
He threatened to disgrace himself by splurgin'.
Women tend to think that man a goon
Who comes not wisely but, instead, too soon.

Of all disappointments who would pick hers
Whose man gets off before he can get in?
But Glenda, when Juan took off her knickers,
Made sure that he knew well when to begin.
To find a happy mean 'twixt flames and flickers
(Though hard when making love is thought a sin)
Is that to which all lovers should aspire:
Only pace and patience can satisfy desire.

For this no graveyard ever was designed.
With Glenda's knickers on a nearby wreath,
Her bra hung on a cross that stood behind,
(I hear the priests and parsons grind their teeth),
The two made merry love, and far from mind
Were those who lay together underneath.
Since sounds of love do not disturb the dead
The grave's a very good place to get laid.

That is a gloomy pun I can't resist.
But anyway I've made it, and that's that.
And now I've reached the climax I'll desist,
For who could follow that and not fall flat?
And yet what bard could bear to end a tryst?
Like Hamlet who said "Now I'll do it pat"
And didn't, this tale I thought I had ended
Ten stanzas back, and then ten more appended.

To write ten more would just be tempting fate.
I'll finish off without undue delay.
The lovers, realising it was late
(The keeper tolled the knell of parting day)
Rose up, and hand and hand walked to the gate.
A woman lost who shows a man the way!
Such irony I trust you'll understand.
So things turn out when woman takes a hand.

End Of Part 3

PART 4

This section will be brief, I guarantee.
It tells of Sean Juan's progress up the ladder
That scaled the walls of University -
And led to one bad boy becoming badder,
There was really little else for him to be.
On reading it some readers might feel sadder,
And wish on Section 4 they hadn't started.
I trust by now those readers have departed.

We left Sean Juan upon the graveyard green,
To be precise, just at the graveyard gate,
More full of life than he had ever been.
Goodbye to Glenda; I'm sorry to relate
(Such power we poets have to change the scene)
She must leave the stage to find another mate.
That noise you hear's the creaking of the winch
That's needed to remove Miss Glenda Pinch.

The confidence of manhood now in flood
It swept our hero quickly to his door.
He passed two friends and gave them each a thud,
His way of saying "I'm a boy no more".
Youth is brashest when it's in the bud.
Excuse me if I mix my metaphor -
It's hard to flower and flood at the same time.
(Except, of course, when looking for a rhyme).

While back at home the Rosary beads were out,
As if his mother had a premonition.
She knew it in her bones, without a doubt -
Her son had cut the cord of his condition.
(An operation Irish men do without
Who from their mothers can not bear division:
The cord of life becomes a Gordian knot
That ties them up forever to the cot).

Sean Juan had tried to get his story straight.
Late for mass, he'd stayed to hear another,
And afterwards had gone to contemplate
(He thought this would really please his mother)
The sermon's meaning. "That's what kept you late?
That meaning must be deep to cause such bother,"
His father said. And Sean replied, "Indeed,
It was about the Sower and the Seed."

But Mr. Juan cared not for Sean's excuse.
I could go on to give his da's reply
In Belfast's vocabulary of abuse -
As long as any list in Rabelais;
And how he thundered on and on like Zeus,
While Mrs. Juan was raining sigh on sigh;
Much as Lord Byron might have spun it -
Least, I think that's how he would have done it.

Instead, I'll take my tale a stage or two.
It was the yearly custom at St. Thomas's
To send a list of all those pupils who
Fulfilled the school's academic promises
By passing their exams and squeezing through
- Over-awing local ignoramuses.
The list was read out from the pulpit's height,
As proof the teaching methods were all right.

The list was always read by Father Bones,
The parish priest who rattled in the aisles,
Beloved by all the districts oldest crones.
His genuflections echoed off the tiles -
They say his knees were hollow, like his moans.
That day his withered face was wreathed in smiles -
Such pleasure in the pass rate (two per cent)
Like the first gum-drop tasted after Lent.

Sean Juan, of course, had missed the great event.
His name was on the list, the very last,
Read out as he dozed to his heart's content
Oblivious, as for many Sundays past.
He had been told what such successes meant:
A job, and opportunities so vast,
It seemed well worth the effort to be made -
A pen is really lighter than a spade.

That <u>was</u> the chief inducement, I'll admit,
That launched our hero on the road to - ?
I wish I could say "success and profit,"
A cosy little bungalow for two,
A pensioned post, teaching English Lit.
To those who've never known an outside loo -
The sons and daughters of the middle-classes,
Who've never felt a cold wind on their asses.

Such were the great rewards his mentors painted,
To make him rise above his lowly station.
For them the streets were damned, the suburbs
   sainted,
Deserving of undying aspiration.
By such ambitions Sean was never tainted,
Never finding dullness a temptation.
An easy life was Sean Juan's only goal,
Avoiding emigration or the dole.

St. Thomas's VP was Sam McSlamm,
Who drove his brighter pupils towards "success",
The sacrifice of the annual exam
Of which he was high priest. So to impress
Father Bones many brains were forced to cram
And cram and cram, until the awful stress,
Aided always by strokes from Sammy's canes,
Had sacrificed another load of brains.

Initiation started each September,
With specimens in classfuls drafted in.
Five days a week he taught them to remember
"To play the game of life you have to win;"
Those who lost he threatened to dismember -
"For useless brains are better in the bin."
Towards the end of May the bins were full,
While Sammy's words still echoed round each skull.

Each day began always with morning prayers.
Six hundred droning boys, still half asleep,
Would mumble, mime and mutter unawares,
Their drowsy eyelids lifted but to peep
At Sammy ranting on the school-hall stairs.
The teachers found it difficult to keep
Their pupils from just falling to the floor
As row by row the school began to snore.

Then after prayers the boys were led away,
And education's mills began to grind,
To process every boy five hours a day,
To fill the slot for which he was designed.
The teachers went to work without delay
Removing any obstacle they'd find.
There were a lot - boys seem to inherit
Such things as "mind" and "character" and "spirit".

Sean Juan was one of those who'd been selected
To study History, Maths and English Lit.,
When many slots had been tried and rejected
Into which our hero simply wouldn't fit.
For several years he was injected
With dates, equations, quotes, and had to grit
His teeth as he learned daily how to cram
Beneath the watchful eyes of Sam McSlamm.

For Maths, Sean Juan was taught by Harry Hogg,
Who loved nothing more than digging out square
   roots;
For History, Sean relied on Clarence Fogg,
Who through the mists of time led his recruits;
For Lit., the budding poet Seamus Bogg -
Each line he wrote it seemed wore water-boots;
Of all things on Earth he loved a puddle,
And wished more words would rhyme with "muddle".

By June his brain was bursting with quotations,
With family trees, and maps, and countless facts
On all the English Kings and their relations,
The ins and outs of Hannibal's attacks,
And Wordsworth's Pantheistic revelations -
Revealed to Sean after a dozen whacks.
Where would the poet be and his refrain
Without the application of the cane?

And as the day approached for the exam
A Mass was offered up by Father Bones,
For God to give a hand to Sam McSlamm,
To help him make hard workers from the drones,
Which Sammy <u>did</u> - by stinging every palm,
Ignoring all of their ungrateful moans.
Alas for Sam! HE did not intervene.
In St. Thomas's GOD was rarely seen.

But when the day had dawned for the attack
Things did not go as well as Sam had planned.
The pupils packed what facts they had to pack
And marched to battle slowly, pen in hand.
A lot of ink was spilt, and mostly black,
So Sammy's little empire could expand.
Too bad it was an awful waste of ink:
His pupils had forgotten how to think.

Sean Juan emerged a little worse for wear.
His pen was empty and his head was sore.
His success his ma attributed to prayer -
Of Rosaries she'd offered up a score.
She didn't know success would lead him where
Opportunities to sin were rather more.
That is, to university - a college
Where quickly he improved his carnal knowledge.

END OF CANTO I.
(TO BE CONTINUED)